CHORUS is a lyric wail stunned into
and personal—though here, as in the
oppositional phenomena. Pieces made

T0267703

and desperate frenzied plea make a rhetoric or salve, or salvation. As the poet
writes, "The songbird is and is not a metaphor./ The songbird is and is not
gone." What I mean to say to you (I meaning me, you meaning absolutely
you, the one reading this) is that this is a book that speaks from a body and
to a body. I felt spoken to. Known. "Are you there. Is anyone there."
—Kazim Ali, judge of the 1st/2nd Omnidawn Book Contest 2021

Tendrilic, electric, Daniela Naomi Molnar's CHORUS traces a mind in
swift action. A near daybook, this collection is intimate and expansive,
born of the solitudes highlighted in the pandemic, while resistant to the
individualisms thrust upon us. It is a choral undertaking that points to the
ecosystems of our languages, the subterranean connections between our
lives and the world, and the "open portals" of books in our current fires. A
stunning book by a poet I am excited to follow.
—Solmaz Sharif, author of Customs

"Whose afterimage am I?" Molnar asks in her striking debut. These poems
interrogate how the self connects and relates to the world around it, and
how these influences shape a larger picture. Each titled "chorus" followed
by a number ("chorus 1/ air" and "chorus 6/ map/ there is no time but
the light remains"), they capture voices in conversation and harmony/
disharmony with each other, "I've noticed how many good hearts have to
stop/ to keep me clothed and fed/ I've noticed the callouses on other hands/
the splinters in paw pads/ the burrs in black feathers that, elsewise, ought
to fly." Writers are frequently invoked, including Bayo Akomolafe ("In this

epoch of porous boundaries, our bodies cannot be considered apart from the stories we tell of them"), Alice Notley, Nietzsche, and W.S. Merwin. Poems about Ojito Canyon ("light advances up the canyon named Ojito, little eye/ black scatter of magpies in deepening blue") provide beautiful descriptions complicated by anxiety, "Worry seeps through the slightest crack. Keep/ the body. Thinking is a truceless act." These poems do not deliver tidy answers to the dilemmas of existence, but rather investigate the division and fragmentation with lyric urgency.

— *PUBLISHERS WEEKLY*

CHORUS

Interior typeface: Garamond
Cover design by Daniela Naomi Molnar
Interior design by Ken Keegan

Library of Congress Cataloging-in-Publication Data

Names: Molnar, Daniela Naomi, 1979- author.
Title: CHORUS / Daniela Naomi Molnar.
Description: Oakland, California : Omnidawn Publishing, 2022. | Summary:
At a time of simultaneous isolation and interconnection, this book is an inquiry into the
edges of the self — where are they, or do they even exist? Pushing back on capitalist dogma of
individuality, CHORUS instead seeks the multiplicitous self, a self that engages the radical
diversity that characterizes any healthy ecosystem or society. Veering between a remote
canyon in New Mexico, the Pacific Northwest, New York City, the virtual world, the past, and
the unstable future, the author asks, "Whose afterimage am I?" The sprawling, celebratory,
mourning chorus of this book is the sum of many voices — the words of other writers, poets,
and artists are interwoven with the author's words. This book is a celebration of the exceptional
capacity of language to supersede bodily limits, mortality, and existential loneliness. This is a
chorus that encompasses violence, love, empathy, fear, a burning planet, a pandemic, heartbreak,
desire, joy, and grief. Each strand in this messy braid is allowed to remain independent and
alive, seeking not resolution but interstices of plurality, discord, and harmony. In this way, a
multiplicity of forms, styles, places, and times are refracted through the lens of a fragmented self,
seeking conviviality and complexity, not resolution.

Identifiers: LCCN 2022038406 | ISBN 9781632431110 (trade paperback)
Subjects: LCGFT: Poetry.
Classification: LCC PS3613.O474 C48 2022 | DDC 811/.6--dc23/eng/20220817
LC record available at https://lccn.loc.gov/2022038406

Published by Omnidawn Publishing, Oakland, California
www.omnidawn.com   (510) 237-5472
10 9 8 7 6 5 4 3 2 1
ISBN: 978-1-63243-111-0

CHORUS

DANIELA NAOMI
MOLNAR

OMNIDAWN PUBLISHING
OAKLAND, CALIFORNIA
2022

One is several, incomplete, and subject to dispersal.

Do you even know / what part of you you are?

…The bright pliancy of human sentience—attention itself—had become the world's most prized commodity, the very movements of our minds transformed into streams of unceasing revenue for someone, somewhere.

In this epoch of porous boundaries, our bodies cannot be considered apart from the stories we tell of them.

Let us beware of saying that death is opposed to life. The living is only a form of what is dead, and a very rare form.

Después // tras la rosa / sombra

The story of the one-legged messenger is that his other leg is walking on the far side of death. "What seems to be over there?" they ask him. "Just emptiness?" "No," he says. "Something before that, with no name."

Whenever I say "I" I mean also "you". And so, together, as one, we shall begin.

1 / FIRE, PROTEST, HEARTBREAK, ISOLATION, AND DISEASE

bare

        inside skin

    trachea   alveoli

wet   whole   need

     brokers

air

               air

air

      declares :   you

air declares :   *you are not*

    free,   *other scenes*

are not   *taking*

place,   *time is not filled,*

                              time is not late

bodies

   are scraps

            rented   meant

        to be   returned

                    war

                              over

Rising sap encased in cambium
the candor of that strict unfinished: *So much elsewhere*
unsettling each surface, so much annulled

> While the hopeless form of the phone
> again finds my hands' helpless hope
> ending only in

I try a new thing:
sourdough succulents showering
believing in god

> An endgame of leftover math
> remaining gaze-locked with solution

I walk to the city's last swamp
A swamp-born whip of a horsetail frond
striped bright green / dark green
rises from black sucking mud
bare branches click above

> I trim my nails
> to the pink quick to dig in the mud
> to add to the catalog
> of all the imperfect
> ways I've loved

let's put this moment

between a scab in the shape of a window
                        & the faint cotyledon

between the hatchet
                        & awareness of the hatchet

between waking bound in white thread
                        & waking bound in red

between the fable
                        & the socket

between the empty shopping cart
                        & asylum

        blanks in a grid   / the cars drive north
        blanks in a grid   / the cars drive south

let's put this moment

between the finger-slicked prayers in a prayer book

             & the intransigent screen

between the cooling coffee

          & normal conditions

between the narrowness wherever the vanishedness touched

           & my own voice cast back off
           anyone else's skin

between the slow-flickering sun

         & deafening continuance

between yellow pine pollen

       & the GDP

     what is lived but surfeit fury of star star star
     or gnawing for a pattern the way photos look true

let's put this moment

between a deadness performing born-ness
                    & the knowledge of being prey
between being prey
                    & praying

        empty pages of a prayer book / metaphor needs a body
        empty pages of a prayer book / simile needs a winch

let's put this moment

between a cluster of black grapes, smooth skins foxed with sugar
                        & a proxy of tenderness,
                        warding off belief
between picking at the splinter
                    & practicing being skin

between a blinking argument of red
                    & a lapse in imminent risk

between breathing
                    & the burst fringe

CHORUS 4 / ELSEWISE

If I can look
this morning at my eyes
what does the rest, elsewise
have to do?

Metronome beat of rain in drainpipe
creamy dogwood bracts pointing all four directions
mourning dove mourning dove mourning
in the zinc-bright rain
a heron flies to the city's last swamp

I've noticed how many good hearts have to stop
to keep me clothed and fed
I've noticed the callouses on other hands
the splinters in paw pads
the burrs in black feathers that, elsewise, ought to fly

Weighted ends of the baton
filled with viscous glitter gel
that I used to twirl up
and down the hot driveway
a march a weft
to weave the spinning

Where's the baton now
cracked plastic, glitter gel
oozes into ocean floor or smears
into chemical heat in some foreign dump
where brown children I'll never, elsewise, meet
walk orbits for what might pay
what might clothe and feed

I've noticed chatty atoms can sustain or kill
and there seems to be no will involved
no ethics or polarity no gauge
I've no grip on that war

So far, today
I've noticed how a nation
can turn its weapons on itself
like I could choose to crush my toe bones to dust
or hole punch my eyes just by looking

Standing in the kitchen eating toast
I tell myself I'm harmless
I only want what I don't have

cantering collapse
and a canter can go on and on and on—straight through what seemed a
wall

...

the man has clear opinions
about lizard aliens and all they can explain
he tells me to bare my feet in the low tide
i obey—it's a new moon
the continent is burning
nobody has a map

...

but what good is a canter
if not for getting lost
i go deep into the smoke
follow the tracks of the desert fox
who follows the tracks of the heron
who follows the water's blue muscles
churning thick with a mixture *of mutiny*
and stringent peace
i go to the far bright hunger dimming

...

meanwhile, time

      prostrates itself to timing

           and ever-smaller breaks break

the full-on hollow

           of looking while looking away

…

it's screaming to us   yet the fire's not angry

      the smoke's not cruel

our cage is elaborate but unsure of itself

      and all its captive ghosts' adorations

         its bars stray

         its bolts rust

           from all the wet mouths

      kissing its docile lock

you hold my head in your hands
in your strong hands my plain head / no target

blaze of amber-crimson-violet heat

a hummingbird swoops to see if my shirt is nectar

swoops

away :   an unfreedom

of air to touch every way / i've lost

the narrative of matter

i've lost your hands holding my head —

i've so little time in my body / my body holds only time
and time only holds my body

if i time my body to your body
will i body my own time
your time in my body / fallow field

you call post-nightmare
to check in on time / you hold

my head in your hands. for a while
you keep holding

as fireweed flares from rock
as miner bees fly from dim rooms
to sun, fly purposive

to the smell of what sustains / *what does not*
change is the will to change
a husk of light / person
from *persona*, mask.

the animals gather seeds   bury them in soil   the animals fatten

my body   your body   impossible   reckonings

with lack or buzzing, blinding   the sun's wounded routes

white rivers of bone   believe it or break   a spine

a salient weed   made in my ossified image   in my presumptions

this itch   this nightmare :   i want   to be found

asterisms crash   to make what myth   what else might a wave

what else   the night   embarrasses   us both

with its bald need for stars   it doesn't need much   just galaxies

2 / OJITO CANYON

light advances up the canyon   named Ojito, little eye
     black scatter of magpies in deepening blue
         two flags trace the wind
   one flag says America   one flag says gold
aspen leaves flicker all the way from the trunk
         i open my palm to the cold day
    but my fingers
   curl slowly in
     a comma a
       soft
       clench to bracket
        the sense
         of this land as
       a lamina of ghosts
         its haunted slivers stacked

    do it right   demands the royal blue bucket under the sink
     do it right   *most curious to me the visible world*
in that it has no motive   when lost in the visible world
     beware bending the map
         be careful around water
      note the eye watching from behind
       the eye that cannot close
   note light's tidal scrutiny
     and the black, shiny eye that cannot close
   not unkind, neither kind   unblinking
  note which direction water flows
away or towards sight

Slow conversion   of self to zero   and in that conversion   advance.

Keep the body   Worry seeps   through the slightest crack.   Keep

the body.   *Thinking*   *is a truceless act.*

Sky pale and brilliant   silhouetting

each juniper   on hills' curved spine.

My body   writes the light.   Sky pinking.   No equation.

All this is life,   *must be life,*   *since it is so much*   *like a dream.*

A cougar in the canyon   flees a cellphone's   light

a coyote curls   in her shallow ochre cave   : *truth stripped*

of its cloak of time   allows the scald of recognition   : the pattern

of this place   a houndstooth weft

row upon row   of biting / being bitten.

The candle spills over   light spreads the dark desk.

Wax pools   moves swiftly to solid   and I want

to tell it, linger.   Allow fluid and partial.

Stay close   to centripetal strange.

I twist the pillar   from its hard puddle.   Resistance then snap.

The sky's gray concavity   a uniform swoop.

Light murmurs provocations.   Light recites the ochre cave.

Light seeps   across all ghosts   into hard spots.

Sky a writhing   lace of flakes   obscuring hills' blue spine.

Sky a cold vertigo.   Keep the body.   A raven lifts

off the aspens' gold   cawing.   Light recites   : additive blur

familiar primitive   tender periphery   fleet.

Imbecile rapacity   says the drained river.

A little nosebleed, always, here.   Dry delicacy of air.

River surge.   Loss clash.   Power gone out.

water   glitches

    in the river

water glitches   in the poem

    voluble, exposed

    air thin enough to hold   mostly

light's   bright breakage

    its branching

ether-folds   of loss   rebuilding things

The centerless tension returns
I try to befriend it
A man's sure movements
a women's hesitant ones
Our ghosts cannot be ousted

Icicle's drape
off roof's turquoise eaves
stretched taut, a clear ligament
will go slack with sun
become pure circulation
will move inside the land
as an *elsewhere of water*, asking
What is closed? What is open? What is a connective path?
What is torn
What is a threshold, a limit

Indigo snow shifts to gilded crisp

Stood yesterday at sunset
in a paw-shaped canyon where the paw pad would be
where the animal would write herself in snow
a crow passed high
amplified silence pushed each wingbeat's whoosh
back to me complete
Lapidary silence
storing each sound
making of it a cup (

Gold cottonwood leaves gone brown
    a wholesale burnishing
        each stung at the petiole by cold's sure claw
            each leaf still clings deadalert

    as the rucked mesa states all visible light
as a self is a fold of forces
    welcoming dialogue, not synthesis
        We move *from pore to star* in a largeness of ourselves

Here to see the pores in the morning's dark skin. Snowmelt light.
    Earth drinking in. Calm like a wasp's nest.

Her eyes, the same pale blue that now rings these red hills. We'd sit on
    swings at night, two sets of new breasts and new eyes, hungry
    to know each other's insides. Night air moved across her soft
    body, air tethered at the apex of the swing—a pendulum
    gathered there, keeping time. As if time is ever kept. Thick
    inner magma, blood locked inside a cage. I'd like to cup your
    warm hip in my hand again, lick the nape of you. We were
    learning to love "woman" despite all we had been told.

We hand back
    our shadows in the end, along with weight, mass, knowledge,
    all belief.
    And to what?
    Palest warmth. A scraggly black
    rooster flaps to a juniper's crook
    preparing to proclaim : all these
    capacities—
    incumbent death's ongoing dodge.
    Retaliatory extravagance bursts from every seam.

I try to out my body's cave like the inside of a sock. I try to listen as
    the cave turns, listen as the damage is warmed and dried by
    time, scabs over, begins to find new form.

Persona : mask—a differentiating principle deployed to hitch a ride
    on perception's *vast inexplicable*, perception's bloody cave.

Persona : mask—on the cave walls, a jargon of ideograms,
    desire lines.

A circle of white lingers below each juniper, untracked
        except by songbirds.
        Songbird meander. Songbird prowl.
        Tiny predator / lucent anchor.
        The land, a lamina of ghosts.
        These bright portals through. Permission slip.

Past moonset, pre sunrise, stars poised on dark hills.

Alone yesterday on a mesa eating handfuls of thirsty snow. Juniper

parched and seeking, a waterghost, a slow-writhing thing. Engraving

water's name. A continuous seeking, I.

Pink wisps now in pale cerulean sky. Hills indigo and umber.

This white far	This breath
This blue far	This breathing
This pink far	This breath
This black far	This edge
This gray far	This lip
	This fold

of each body, a map of contact. Of relinquishment and hold.

I drift out from the canyon's inlet, trace again the world with sight.

I try to see my own edges. Trace where I become all else. To feel the me

and the not-me align in that reprise.

as when an otherwise / Opens in the body

I split along the seam of my own perfect damage.

Like a rock in a riverbed cracked by water's scrutiny, water's dash, water's

deletions, its radical excisions, its unsealing, its tunneling, its certain

tongue, water's irregular questions, water's habitable script.

Water's ears reeling, water's eyes contriving, bewildered, this slender

breakage and drift —

Glimpses are signatures.

The ghosts live me.

The flag in the valley maps the wind like my eyes map the seam of me,
     moving.

...

I was taught to sew seams in a second-story room, the smallest in the
     house, in a brownstone in Queens. Running my fingertips
     along the skeins of embroidery thread again and again to feel
     their silky colors touch my skin, listening to the spin of the
     black iron sewing machine, spinning, spinning... and the
     closet with its torn plastic bags of fabric scraps, all potentials.
     No plan, just belief. My grandmother's beaten hands guiding the
     machine that could join or sunder, that could script a strong,
     pliant unity of two separate things or could tear into a hand.
     That could patch or puncture, and must puncture in order to
     patch. No seam without the thousand tiny holes to hold
     the thread.

The black thread, the white thread, the red thread, the green, tan,
     brown, violet, yellow, pink. The blue thread. The pale blue,
     the dark blue, thread to match the fabric it remade. Stitches
     meant to be unseen. And unlike the stitches in a wound
     which vanish into skin's inherent holding, these stitches
     stayed, binding matter to itself, making folded form. To
     clothe and warm a body, to contain.

Each day, reseal the seal

    between self and not-self

    badly so it's porous, fidgets or shimmers

    when asked to stay quiet

    when asked to stay contained.

He's dark water, unstill. Seeped into me : total hunger / total

    surrender. The body is infinite. Slept beside him soundly,

    listening to the rain.

The materiality of the body is one way to get free. The begonia leaf,

    another : sun on iridescence : warmth, connection, food.

    The desert's quiet methods for storing all that falls.

This land of *habitable scars* in which I try to see convictions as

    they taper.

I watch all discernables turn cureless, scatter, clash.

    in a field

    I am the absence

    of field

    or

    the field is also me

    and I am also the field

    which means

in a field

I am the presence

of field

and the perception

of field

and the field felt

by field

and the field seen and smelled

by field

the field

known by field

as paltry and honest

a knowing

as knowing can be

which is a type of love, a type of killing, a type of warmth,
connection, food. A type of conviction. A stray fold,
attention-ironed until crisp.

...

Another sunrise and this canyon cups the light into gold. Roof rust is
    written, a story told through precipitate and ice. I fixate on
    the roof's rivets, each an arced galaxy, each a silver dome
    holding a circle of captive sun.
As a co-metabolic mammal, I peer into a mirrored spring whenever I
    try to see.
So much for the autonomous and pure.
So much for the conjuring of lonely breakage, all removes.
So much for the I as a hollow in our shared tensile web. That old
    battlefield's gruesome cipher has nothing that needs, now,
    to be told. Cease your lonely winter. Sole warrior, lay it down.

...

When I felt, as a child, a sense of the not-self entering my perception,
    I felt it as a comfort, not an assault.
When I saw the men praying, their suit-clad dark backs rocking to and
    fro, eyes closed, muttering Aramaic to smooth books in worn
    hands, I knew that their eyes were rolled back in their skulls,
    seeing into that density, the brain's many banishments and
    conjurings, a neural map of shrapnel/restoration, a
    technology of hunger and hunger's reprieve.

Time skitters, spreads, languishes—like water, like time.

I clasp fast the marker of another cobalt dawn.

The brain, a technology of hunger and hunger's reprieve.

In the desert, I think of my distant city where noise bloats the air.

traffic, n. : traced back far enough :   *touch repeatedly, handle;*
                                                       go beyond, rub, break

Touch repeatedly, break. Go beyond, break. Break, rub, break. Touch
      repeatedly, break. Once broken, I am entered. Filled by a not-
      self. As I've been taught. Learned helplessness —

Full morning light here. Keep the river / keep the river /*shockwaves of*
      the mind

There is no time
but the light remains.

Noise as thought *slides as fever in the veins* inside the silent morning.

...

Noise, a type of grief. Grief, a type of love.

I wrench my mind back to the color of the hills, palest green.

At the noise's center, what? Nodes, attempts — or symbioses,
      darknesses — or awarenesses' awareness, history writ twice
      — a swarm of animal intelligence, uprooted, thrown —
      a sponge of anyways, besides — a mopping up of origins —

a hunger always onç

Quotidian violence is no less violent, no less deadly to what swaths
might still sustain.

I'm trying to insist. My attention, long since logged to a nub. I'm
trying, with all my faulty skin, to encompass, to be, the map's
cacophonous key.

Pre-dawn. I nudge the wick from its fetal curl, create light.

Pink clouds this morning with cerulean and cobalt, lavender and gray.
Like all light, it passes, it's past. Wispy now, fringed peach.

The clouds chorus the sky. Narrate and translate, turn to story,
then belief.

...

hurt pathways of thought : A thought is hurt by becoming a belief.
Overuse, a walking stick's metronomic stab.
The pathway scabs,
gags on belief debris,
clots into a road.
A road is a path that's been smoothed by speed, become belief.
My life, my mind,
bulldozed, paved
then clawed, winnowed
from belief back to path.
The person on that path dissolves into a charge when a touch draws
near.

...

Today the world has less living. Replaced with roads, concrete,
   mortar, heat.
   Due to increased structure, the world has more shadows.
   To hide in. To obscure. To read like light can be read—
   ragged, aloud. Sometimes true.
   Each day, light and shadow create the world anew.
   Stay with me, move slowly now, see
   how each atom of matter is somehow rendered visible,
   sometimes even touchable, sometimes even knowable or
   feelable—scented or tinted, solid or fluid, flung to touching,
   feeling, calling back—

Like the call of the owls flanking the creek where I hiked last night,
   dark falling fast and with it, pure cold. Trail turned to ice. My
   feet fumbling for a hold and I saw a cougar clamp down on
   my neck. Then the owls spoke. A call-and-response across the
   creek's song—creek's chorus, owls' hook.

A sound	like a magnet gone ether.
A sound	like the absence of sound.
A sound	like sound's shadow.
A sound	like the overthrow of matter
	a numinous, stern affirmation that yes
	life is immaterial, these wings,
	a stopgap tool and so are those
	dumb hands.
A sound	of the seam between.
A sound	affirming nothing, denying nothing,
	surging, keeping the dark ajar —

I decide again to witness. Language, maps, icy paths.

Each footfall, a foil for my knowledge of nothing.

Footfall as knowledge, footfall as belief.

The patience of the story is unparalleled.

The story waits just like a story, knowing it will be told.

...

The flag in the valley still traces the wind, saying *america america* no
        matter how
it torques, billows, clumps, catches, falls into folds.
Riddled with bullet holes, sodden with blood.
That flag, beyond shame. Long poisoned by the commonest venom.
That flag, clear and clean in the desert morning light.
Writ by the storied wind, shadow cast across the road.

Last night I lay in bed inching limbs north, syncing with the earth's
spin to maximize moonlight. Steeped silver   — until a mundane
memory suddenly sparked fear, and in that fear, shatter : perception
snatched and trapped inside memory's box
where no moonlight could touch.

Memory is a trespass that shatters and makes identity.

Identity, easily shattered, a leaky greed
in need of resealing, ceaseless.

Water brings energy
the way memory creates identity.

water becomes life   memory becomes identity
water becomes identity   memory becomes life
life becomes memory   memory becomes identity
identity becomes water   water becomes life

Water's memory is all there is of life.

Made and brightly shattered : shattered and brightly made.

After the shattering, the spirit remains. After the shattering, the soul.
After the river, the river's flickering skin.
After the river, all it feeds, fills with memory. *One's life is one's home.*

51

Dispose of any map. Read the river by the light it traps, casts back.

I want the light of the moon to be remembered

by the spots it couldn't touch.

What holds the shadow still holds.

To see a thing
only for what
it physically is, is

its own distortion.

The toppled

clawfoot bathtub's

feet poke from

the brush

behind the shed

like helpless hooves

of a tipped cow.

The tub's chipped

white convexity

the cow's belly, belly up.

Every time I see it

I want to untip

the cow.

Stars' final tatters constellate the day. Stars are bones. Day, a
      stubborn muscle.
One car's headlights trace the road into town. My mind's tide pulls
      back—jagged black rocks. Pulls back, advances. Memory
      snaps into place alongside vision. *A rough and intricate hazard*
      of perception, performed each moment, for no audience
      but oneself.

...

Two days into ambiguous terrain. The ignominious sociopath says
      victory, the other rallies for ongoing math. We citizens go
      about our days, masked or unmasked, thumbs pressing and
      flicking smooth responsive glass a little more often than the
      day before. The one who has won is whoever owns those
      thumbs' orbit.
An ordinary spreading of my pockets on the dark table, not seeing
      how air bends around the edges of each humdrum form and
      stays there, breathing.
Be astonished : gum wrapper.
Be astonished : dust.
Pressurized perception—this is political, too.

...

The compass quivers northward toward my home where I am a burnt
forest. Where even my seedheads are ash. Where I've lost
entirely the grip of anything certain, no traction against the
slide. What holds a consciousness together

other than breath's metronome. Every day, another
treacherous language to decode. Every day, another
hallucinatory loneliness to unravel. Every day, another
banishment from the clarity of purpose, all edges gone gauzy
in a patina of fear.

Look just beyond the well-marked road, its yellow lines, their
placental directive.
Use your mutinous orb of eye.
Wake, each day, in the dark, seeking. Find what you find
alone. *If anything is alive there is no such thing as repetition.*

...

Yesterday, I ran around a paved track in this canyon eleven times. No
owls called. I was not in danger of being mauled by a cougar.
And no enchantments found me either, only exercise. A
routine stating only that its contents must be read differently
each time. And again, with less sleep. And again, recklessly.
And again, with hunger. By the river. By the juniper's slow
writhe. By the need, again, for distraction. With the
blasted land.

Some amount of loss is fuel but I'm tired of its taste. It tastes like the
entrails of wind through a plastic window. It tastes like
boxed sky.

The ghosts beg for essence, the ghosts beg for oatmeal, the ghosts
       won't shut up about makeup tricks and optimizing time.

The ghosts are stuck on grossing

the next bright way to crash.

The ghosts are galvanized neglect.

The present fury is ash. What of ash : amending soil boosting
your lawn add ash to your home compost wood ashes for
cleaning make soap at home keep harmful bugs away add
traction to slippery paths soak up driveway spills fire control

                                    Ash as fire
control : a self negated by a negated self. *So many plurals and
veerings, so much away* —

...

A coyote in a vast caldera, evanescing calm, black ears perked above
       gold grass. She listens to the faint frequency of chaos, a
       murmuring her paw pads understand. A disinterest
       in mistake.

The coyote's tail in the caldera, tilted up and waving.

The tail of a morning constellation poised on the mesa's black lip.

The coyote is a dog, a free dog, synonymous with wild.

A linguistic confession that we construct

mostly cages. Outside the storycage,

life is scattered spurts of simultaneous / overlap / repeat /

...

Bits of waxen exoskeleton undo the candle's form, softening off. Sky
        begins to blue. Cinnamon coffee. Weather blowing in.
I am the background. The sky, fore. I am the spacious non-entity. I am
        the limit case.
The void is an exuberance of political importance.
Matter is metaphor : only varied entanglements constitute all nouns.
Matter is metaphor : all matter is a finger pointing at the moon. Look
        at the moon.

The candle has collapsed itself warmly. Smoke spirals in whorls from
        the wick. Matter is metaphor : everything a partial story of
        itself, unfinished because unfinishable.
        The sky goes cotton candy all at once
        over rucked red rocks of mesa
        crimping eons in each fold.

We tangle with eternities with every perceptual stab. Every wagered touch
    brushes against *exuberant transience.*
        The shroud of my mouth
        tries to contain the juniper
        that ancient, edgeless being
        will not still inside its name.

...

Da Vinci held a pane of glass perpendicular to the world, one dark dot
        at its center in order to construct a story of stable seer and
        seen. Meanwhile, the glass itself flowed. That one dark dot,
        the root and sum of so much simplifying violence. That dot
        really ought to have been erased by now—or at least
        smudged to a shadow that might alter the lucidity of the
        world but cannot determine its story, its sense.
        I lose the thread of my thoughts.

        This is why the dot persists, why and how we keep ourselves
        central.

        My mind drifts into lists, the churning stories used to bolster.
        The stories are sordidly quotidian, insurance against eternity.
        Eternity can wait while this meeting gets a color-coded slot.
        The digital paperwork's more pressing than the need for
        a soul.

Without a stable self in a storied world, convictions perforate
        beyond use.

Moving into this rich wreckage can feel like violence.
Its just a generosity too large for us to know.

...

58

Particles shiver when magnified but they are not cold or scared. The unstable void isn't searching for a map.

Cold canyon wind slices through old glass. My hand that holds the plastic of this pen and the pen and the ink that streams from its tip and the paper onto which it flows—and the spine in my body, coccyx to sacrum to brainstem to brain—and the muscles that hold it emplaced, and the ruddy light now on the canyon's lip, and my own lips, parched and aging and aching to be kissed—and my heart, the actual organ, compressing and expanding over and over again— all metaphors of matter. Impossible to constrain. All, too, also, nameable and named. Able to act. Capable of force and sometimes intention. Capable of attention. Look for a capsized door.

I feel my dead grandmother move my hand to my head and gently scratch my scalp : matter dips and weaves like an ouzel in a dappled creek,

traceless.

And all this indeterminacy? It looks just like the world.

Shifting, shifted, always yet to shift. Thick with transience, masked with symbol.

A wool shirt rests upon my lap

        : heavy, tight-woven, tan, tough seams, gold snaps
        : a gift from a man I once loved, moth-weight incantation
        : carries the factory that formed it, the hands of the worker who sealed seams, checked symmetry, then moved to the next wool shirt, a procession of samenesses...
        : upon inspection, shirt shatters. Shards everywhere—

and its heft, entire, simultaneous, warm upon my thighs, made *of molecules and lament / where an intelligence lives.* Like the air seems to snap shut the edges of a thing but breathes there, dreaming.

...

A sun-cooked caldera where a black-eared coyote
settles her head between her paws and rests, tail up.
Feels the sun on her back and breathes.
This isn't prayer. Facts
are useful to me she said
because I have no stories in my head.
And what, pray, is the difference.

I dream of my friend on his island, his view of the ocean's heft
origin-whipped wind   touchable, unknown.
He sees an upturned bell of water trying still to ring.
His life moves into memory, all his paintings pressed with precision into
storage space.

...

Morning sky like an absentminded, gentle touch. The cloud's pink
fingers trace the sky's blue back. Driven by a soft motor other
than a mind.
Yesterday, two signs on my hike:

WILL FLOOD WITHOUT WARNING

Are we ever warned of the flood. Do we ever know what is
overtaking us or when we'll be overtaken.

Preceding that, ALL WITHIN IS PROTECTED

*every man/every woman carries a firmament inside / & the stars in it
are not the stars in the sky.*

All within is protected

tunneling through entropy like memory of —

the Lincoln Tunnel, orange sodium lights every 23
feet. Traffic unmoving, as always. As always, horns.
A jut of citizenry below the water's weight. I wonder
about air, scarcity of. I wonder about bombs, about
heat sensors and checkpoints and skin color and
skin. Inside skin of lungs, formerly pink, caked with

exhaust and mold, lungs suspended between states :
NJ / NY : water / air :

real below dream : below dream : below dream :

every passenger in every car, a separate anxious
language. Every idling car carrying within an
expectation of arrival and awareness that arrival will
continue to recede. No one wants to catch anyone
else's eyes through the auto glass though we sit,
unmoving, close enough to touch, captive in a woven
cove of ordinary-strange.

A *fragile imaginal cloth* holds the tunnel down, holds us all as traffic.

Traffic : to touch repeatedly, to break.

A *fragile imaginal cloth* holds us, unbudging chasms

full of desire to be not present, to be not visible, to be not seen
    through the auto glass.

Binary ratcheting up.

...

Everything arrives energetically, at first. I keep finding
songbird's rumps
tail feathers dusted red
wing feathers spread
what flesh there is
eaten or re-arrayed by time.
The storm brought the songbirds down.

The songbird is and is not a metaphor.

The songbird is and is not gone.

...

To feel is to give oneself over

to matter's metaphor

to relinquish doubt's spin, for a spell.

I feel a bird on a power line look down at me.

Another storm approaches

like a cougar threading through rock

dis- or re-appearing when and how she decides.

The songbirds brought down the storm.

In some cultures, day begins at sundown so dark marks day's start.
    When light comes at dawn, it's a midway marker, a lapse of
    light in the originary dark.

Belief frames the day. Last night, wind and tiny whips of rain lashed
    corrugated steel and old cracked glass. The night's icy rain
    seeps now deeper, feeding juniper roots, sage roots, pine
    roots, cedar. Remakes small arroyos, turns them back to clay,
    sculpts red gullies that held, all night, the dark and hold, now,
    the day.

    Malleable, rivuletting, carved by water's authoritative hands :
    all is witness and hive. In cities last night, dancing and honking
    and screaming in the streets. In this canyon, an iron gong was
    rung once, its sound bouncing off the canyon walls then up
    into the sky.

...

I appear, a groggy conduit. Here, I am here, offering perception. What
    else can I give?

A reckless and partial translation of perception to language,
    perception to art.

If a path is held ajar a blink too long or a lifetime too long—glance
    back and the path will be a road. The *fragile imaginal* upwelled,
    riven.

...

For now the world forms, stacking its shapes like blocks. Here, an
    ancient mesa. Here, a low cloud painted peach and lime
    green. Here, thin white sky. Here, a filigree of juniper.
    Here, a rusty roof. Sunday morning and the village sleeps.
    Palest flicker of a star, teetering between made-up and made.

Entity contact : I ask the star if what's gone might not be totally gone. If
    the web might stay fed and taut enough to fix more sensation
    to sensation. A desire like wind, changing everything by
    touch.

Why am I here at 5 am every day. Because this is how I want to live.

Willingness and will. Because each attempt matters. Better be sure
    that's true.

I keep reappearing here in order to appear.

The world means exactly what it means and its meaning is also always
    doubled

refracted back as myth. How to navigate this luminous, how to start
    each day in the dark.

There are places time pleats // so discontinuous moments are

      pressed convivial.

              I walk through pleats

    feel their density

              feel how gravity is tractioned

    by time tugging time

              feel my steps slow —

what unit, what instrument might measure this force.

The imagination, alone.

Feeling is the only way to access some realities.

Walking and feeling : each a *move into*. I move into the star. I move into
      love. I move into the room, tap the door's turquoise jamb. I
      move into the horizon's quilt of gray clouds, feel its gullies
      and whorls.

I walk the canyon's road and see a splinter of sunlight on the tips of
      mesa trees—for a moment, then gone, like an admission or
      mistake. Does the world make mistakes? The splinter
      reappears on rock, closer now, then disappears again. It will
      reappear next south of here, behind me.   I won't see it.

That slice of light : perception yields sometimes a
concentrate of what's received.

Orange juice concentrate in my childhood freezer—its slick,
cold tube. You're supposed to add water to it and—*I will I
will* —but first let me lick this frozen sweet straight to my
hot brain! Neurons glitter into action. The world, so bright,
such sweet splintered light—

that sugar, a pleat. A redoubling that lets more, for a
        moment, in.

    Then the resealing. From the door opposite mine, the smell
        of vodka wafts. My friend was drunk again last night. We
        chase dilation, try to move into thick clarity or blur.

If I light a fire to stay warm, the crease of time widens. I am allowed
        into the pleat between knowledge and heat, *between meaning
        and force, between the idea and a body.*

...

A diffusion of dissonance made by space : this is the desert's power.

The desert is absent presence   /   present absence.

                                Desert space quiets

                the tumult of light

           spreads it slow

      warm fat on dry toast of land.

Desert air

    a sustenance nourishing as tallow.

The desert doesn't need to be seen.

I see, leagues away, the individual branches of individual trees growing
        silently on the mesa. Entering into the oddity of matter, I
        find its unbreachable strangeness, feel my legs stretch across
        the chasm

of perception and fact.

Time pleats—where's my shadow cast?

Only into the chasm.

Trace it, find the juice, its blinding

sweet-tart

decades on, still tastable.

...

Whose afterimage am I?

I look for a capsized door. Go through it, tapping its turquoise jamb,
tasting the iron of rusted hinges as they squeal open then
shut. If you've come this far, the coffee has gone cold—
keep coming. Beyond the door, a vascular river. Check the
altimeter. Cross-reference the chart. A hypsometric map has
been provided. Unfold its crisp pleats and a creased place
is told.

A lead line is weighted for making depth soundings. Sound out the
depths of this chasm. Spool the length of line, coil it round
one hand. Its weight a dollop of concentrated space, a
flourishing of mass, embalmed, like you, by gravity. Its heft,
a pleasure, dropping into the dark.

I've never seen this before, I remind myself, seeing again the blueing sky.

Through the adobe walls, the sleep-coo of a bird.

The anxiety of leaving here lessens me, makes me smaller. I'm returning,
though, freer than I left. Free : trace it back, find *priy-a* : dear,
beloved. From there, to *pri* : love.

The white church spire where the valley's body becomes a neck, near
what's signed as "ruins," otherwise known as the remnants of the
people who reciprocally tended this place for generations, lived in
homes built to be warm in winter, cool in summer, dark in the
desert sun—built of the red earth that fed them in all ways, kept
them free.

Until that church was built, white as starlight, taller than anything. Which
made the houses squat and stained and lumpy, which made the
people, suddenly, brown.

The bird's sleep-coo ceases as the white light ascends.

Sunlight presses shadow down into canyon while the tide of light laps the
mesa's gold lip.

I'm getting rearranged by all the seeing and being seen.

no way

to predetermine reception

...

The violence of the city grid and in it, my house, to which I will soon
return. Below that house are infinite fine lines, tributaries that
feed the region's rivers.

There was a man, not so long ago, who determined it best to bury those
waters to build human homes. I imagine, daily, clawing into the
cold clay to free the buried creeks. Because they were buried alive,
they haunt. They stare at me unblinking. Up through my floors,
through the cage of my ribs, the aspirational confidence of my
upright spine. They see into my brain, that shadowed mass, riven
by *meander lines*. Like the lines that the tributaries want again to
freely trace.

What good is this haunting.

Its weight in me, a bias, a sag, a permanent bent desire. A *silent,
vertiginous sliding*.

Here I am, a slid node.

A broken integument of time, *rearranged by all the seeing and being seen*.

...

I think of Christine.

no way

to predetermine reception

I don't want to but I think of the gun and her head. I think of my mom
calling me when she learned. I had just parked my car and started
the walk under the howl of the freeway so her voice was barely
audible in the chaos of my ears. My mom's fast, frantic voice spun
small questions, small questions — to avoid seeing the gun.

Christine's was an ordinary female white American life. Her suffering,
unremarkable.

The two of us as naked girls on the summer dock, our dangling feet tracing
the lake's cool skin. Humid sunset air buoying the laughter of our
mothers from somewhere in the house.

Her suffering, so ordinary it could not be seen.

Opacity isn't a measure, ever, of truth.

The gun made her suffering both visible and dead.

My life as an automaton underneath that freeway and my mother faint
and frantic in my ears. Christine screams, perhaps at me. I run.

Our little kid feet, the water, the sun going down. Stars through the
blueing air. Butter on a corncob being grilled nearby. Christine,
your hair was soft, fine, gold—how I envied it. Your small,
delicate bones made me feel like an ogre. My jealousy, just one of
many weapons you walked straight into, smiling distantly. Inside,
you had gone dim, rum-soaked, gridded. Your body kept the tally
of mild, agreeable, pretty, invisible, slender, full of rage.

Christine, you are a casualty in the war against the imagination.

All of the other ways you might have been seen.

Our mothers' distant laughter and our toes tracing the lake

a gentle sleepy lapping, rippling, ripping out.

Again, this rancorous map?
I'm sick of its far-off train horn, its dumb, ominous dark. I'm sick
of its female moon. I'm sick of its poisoned implications, its sad,
stubby trees. Can't we get a tree that doesn't tattle on the trouble?
A childlike tree with lime green leaves, thick-barked and straight-
spined with ever-upturned hands.

The cold sky gathers its light, shows again

the frost-darkened rosebush by the stucco's small rupture

next to the power gauge that keeps fritzing out.

The unremarkable wall with its unremarkable crack

to which my attention continues to return.

Habits of perception which constitute a "self" I fear and protect.

The compass didn't move all night but stutters now into spin.

The map grew again through a lock.

All night in raw cold, my dreams swelled their skins

stretched translucent and hideously smooth.

I stood below them, waiting for the burst.

I woke when the child next door

asked questions to the dark

to which he didn't want honest answers.

Are you there. Is anybody there.

...

I'm desperately in love with this place and I'm about to leave, return to a
        life, a place, I don't understand. Cold gold light on the mesa.
        Flint and clay and dust. In order to understand hardness, consider
        further the depth and length of each scratch. Evidence is all
        around. Rocks cool quickly and contain mostly glass.

Let's discuss again the situation. My dense, polluted industry of mind, a
        plangent malice. Let me try again. I'll dispose of the restlessness
        with both broken hands. I'll not glance once at the long-gone
        ingenue, her particular waiting, her milky-eyed equanimity.

I'll be instead curious of this hollow, its cultivated doom. There's
        an innocent voice at the bottom of this canyon asking for a
        foothold. I'll hold up my palm, press its storied folds against the
        sternum's voice, say, here, I am here.

My palm's life line wrinkles into gaps.

The morning sky is carved into curved rills of clouds.

I can't seem to whittle into anything short of diatribe.

I didn't expect a strict order but nor did I expect a wholesale
smashing up.

Isn't there a story in which the animals outshout us?

I want the one in which the core of the story is neither betrayal
nor pat coherence.

I see instead the hollow and say it over again.

...

The subway surfaces halfway home to Ditmas Park. I could keep
going to Brighton Beach — there's water there, and sand — but I
get off at my stop, nod at the friendly Jamaican men who ignore
me by now, another distantly friendly white girl, another self-
delusional member of the gentry. I walk three blocks home where
my roommate follows her orange cat around, whisking up fur and
turds. In my room, big, old windows. Apparently stable frames
on the world. Leafless maples branch and branch again. Orange
streetlight slicks the cold street. I'm 28. I make paintings in that
room that nobody will see. They're strange and beautiful; they
excavate a story I don't yet understand. They will be hidden flat in
a flat file when I am 41.

Every day, the same lunar weather.

Language's abscesses and capillary hairs. It drinks

up the earth because what else is there to drink.

Drinks the din of the animals trying to outshout us.

Knowledge of the void is knowledge of fullness. So I'll just let

equanimity sheds its skin. A costume, after all, not a disguise.

Let's allow transmutation to run laps round ennui.

We can wish, without waiting, for heroic times.

Forms turn deep

> as gray light gathers in the canyon's red fold.

The light is charged, regenerative, generous. Its surges through me and
I become less slack, more tuned. Tensile, not tense. Ready to sound
gravity, allure, origin.

> My body's mold, a temporary home for the reverb,
> the verb, of this gray-turning-blue as the impatient
> dead move smoothly through.

The sky now radiant, a clear sweep from lavender at the apex to turquoise
at the mesa.

> A line of clear light drops into the canyon, to
> rearrange there.

...

The imaginal is *a realm superseding individual volition.* Largest not-me,
  not-mine.

To create a soul, translate imaginal to imaginary.

I/you am a sieve of the imaginal. Imaginal shadowbox.

Each day, we sequester, release, arrange, re-contain.

Each day, we become a brief instantiation of the world thinking itself.

The day thinks us into form. We bend light and time slightly this way,
  slightly that.

Each of us a limited infinity like the ocean in meander lines.

A bathymetric map plots a water body's bottom. A bathymetric map
    listens in order to see. Everything is audible. Each sonic
    fragment radiates, is thrown. *Thrownness* : we arrive where we
    arrive—in a body, in a life—not by accident but by force.
    We are hurled into being, which implies a hurler. Or maybe
    we're both hurler and hurled. Reciprocal topology. Even
    rocks once flowed.

...

Pull these abstractions, like breath, into a memory mold.

The far edge of Portugal, riding a rented bike alone. I'm 27, done with
    school, self-flung to the fringes of a continent to pedal into wind.
    Bright, reticent wooden doors with heavy wooden crosses. The
    bald tires of the bike roll along the cobblestones. Slick matter on
    slick matter, interspersed with speed. I might've, but didn't, crash.

Nobody else is around. Sky, gulls, sea, wind : blue, black, white. The
    westernmost tip of Europe or the easternmost tip of the sea. The
    wind is sharp as the black rocks and their shadows. I wander
    down each side street. Each dead ends in a cliff shearing off into
    the sea.

    Aimless, uncoiling an extremity of myself.

    What is known knows the knower.

    A mesh of the imaginal careens the mold of me.
    Which is also the historical, which does not subside.

        Unsubsided : gnostic heresies imagined three
        types of humans—pneumatic, psychic, hylic.
        The hylic were unredeemable, only good for
        slaves. The pneumatics were angelic, saved or
        nearly so.

Unsubsided : Aristotle's "climate theory" and Alcidamas' refutation. Aristotle claimed that different climes made for different human grades. Lesser grades could be treated as higher grades saw fit. An equally prominent philosopher of the time, Alcidamas disagreed, said all people should be free. Whose name do we now know.

Unsubsided : Gomes de Zurara, paid by the King of Portugal to make the King's uncle, a slaver, look like a good guy. Zurara gazed at the slaves fetched from Africa, each captive a different color, caramel to coal, coming as they were from vastly different ethnicities and tribes. Zurara felt sure that enslaving those people of *bestial sloth* would improve their lives. Hatred as salvific, enslave to save.

Unsubsided : the Doctrine of Discovery : if you are not Christian or if you are not white, you are not fully human and therefore shall become the property of the Christian whites in order, of course, to save your needy soul.

A lamina of trauma : land, body, air.

To create your soul, translate imaginal to imaginary. Unsubsided :
    soul murder.

The imaginal molded into bullet, bible, shackle, skin color chart, slave
    ship, whip, gas chamber, dog trained to kill.

The imaginal translated to imaginary, but translated wrong—*is it a*
    privilege to inherit a death-driven system that maims and constrains?
    Is it a privilege to inherit that mold-turned-cage in which
    everyone—everyone—can only grow deformed?

...

Jeno's baby blue Plymouth slices through July heat, my brother
    and I in the sticky backseat, no seat belts, small bodies tumbling
    back and forth across the wide expanse, banging into each other,
    screams of delight all the way to Jones Beach where the sun trails
    cadenced water, where we eat melted babka and tomato salad
    flecked with pale sand. Jeno's face is vacant, wide, very pale,
    unsmiling in the sun. I reach for his huge hand, clutch one finger.
    He doesn't seem to notice.

Jeno's first wife and babies and the earth itself, its patient seasons and cool watery seep — all had been burned — bones snapped and turned to smoke, barley yanked from the dirt, roots dangling.

My father was hurt by this hurt man.

In turn, my father hurt his children.

This story is so blindingly linear

that it's easy to forget. *Gray surrounds us and we ignore it.*

Gray light gathers in the canyon's red fold to rearrange there.

Gray light, the imaginal. Seeing/not seeing it, the soul.

...

What has subsided? Does anything subside?

...

Cruising two-wheeled along the traumatized continent's edge, feeling free, feeling unmolded from the map of my father and my father's father...

Jeno liked to build things. All his tools were bad, brought from the old country. A metaphor and not. All were busted, cheap to begin with then used beyond use. Squeaky, rusted, chipped, dusty.

Before his wife and children were murdered by men who imagined them a different race, he had been a peasant, a man who farmed and owned a bar because he never drank. On the other side of the war, a hollow terror kept living, looming over his own life.

He made a cutting board I own. It's crooked and rough. I use it mostly for fruits because it's small, just the right size for splitting an apple, for cutting out its core.

Pink light in ribs, asking again how to see.

        Inquires as to the shape of wind.

                      A good question

        highlights a rupture in the bathymetric map.

        I've listened hard in order to see. But what is seen

asks back.

Ribs gone gray, shifted north.

             Yes, he said to me, I'm pushing you away.

             What else is there to say?

I'm pushing you. Ribs crack. Fragments flung

        against the dome. Why trust anyone, ever.

    Because the flag in the valley

            trust-traces wind.

    Because rust

            trust-traces corrugation.

    Because an abacus of trust.

            Because a life lived without trust

is a sad life to live.

So I lay my whole body flat
in the icy river
until I can't ask.

His body shook even when he was still. Which means he was never still. I saw this as a sign of his enchanted, creative agitation. Later, it was a sign of his shiftiness, his shadiness, his inability to sit even with himself.

Ribs weft-grown, east-pressed, dissolve.

Small birds in the thicket unbutton the air with song.

Pushed away, thrown, I go inside the tree. I find the cambium beneath the
bark where no one is in charge. Where silence is speech and
communion. Where what is hidden is hidden only to protect.
Hidden can be wingspan.

Pushed away, thrown, I go to the riverbank, its capillary bleeding feeding
all the cottonwoods and rodents, night visitors with round
black eyes.

The cottonwoods' gray, twining muscles trace water and light,
another form of trust.

A few yellow leaves cling, dainty-edged with scallops, crisp as
aphorism.

Today I will cut the tips of my hair.

I will set these strands on a cottonwood leaf to float down the river,
out of sight.

An act of refuge from linear logic, its brutal neutral gaze.

...

Pushed, thrown to the edge of my private void.

I peer into the black mud to see my dented path but there's not
enough light.

Have I walked here? Flown?

Compass in continual spin.

There's no language here. I can look or look away. My eyes, in looking, can be open or closed. *Let the earth drop away inside your belly falling falling until you're left in space—*

> I'm a fetal curl in a small white space. The fetus drops out of me in a thick current of blood. Nobody else saw this because nobody wanted to see. *Write this. A word may be shaped like a bed, a basket or tears or an X—*
>
> Write this. With that blood was not just
>
> the one life that never will be lived
>
> but the billions of lives untouched by that life. Write this.
>
> > I.
> >
> > Write this.
> >
> > I walked out into the garden and buried
> >
> > your one life there.
> >
> > The hellebore ate you and is now your shape.
> >
> > I left that garden and I left you, too.

The void river gallops away, a black coursing lidded with light. A dead
    baby is not a metaphor.

I had to leave. I had to leave.

I left not the fact but the fact's unceasing recitation in enclosed space.

...

Return to the hair. Each strand
will be blown off the leaf to cast its own thread of shadow
through the water to the water's musculature.
Each thread of shadow will be seen not just by the water
but also by the hive inside the watercourse. By its fractures and dams.

The shape that lives instead of you.

One shape like a small, unremarkable stone.

One shape like a seam that is threshold and gash.

What shuts, what opens.

For your persistent overgrowth, I enclose within a lock.

I promise : no honesty

is its own starvation.

Chipped bones of the world, shaken out and scattered,

landed in red dirt.

Sky is a wholesale

vanishing of mind / I quarry the sky for story.

I wait in blades of shadow then pounce on logic like a cat.

Play with my prey. Consider its innards and how they might serve

the person being constructed by all this predation.

Sky is a churning instrument of worldsped wind.

Cold wind through old glass.   The candle convulses.

Wind is invisible   except in all it touches.

Touches everything.

And in touching, re-forms.   The rock,

the skull, the skin—truth-like translations.

The storm's insouciant stare as I quarrel

    with my brain blood, try to choose

        the opposite of memory, a type of seeing

            I've merely glimpsed

          before the mind's swift winnowing.

    I try to trace a line of shadow as it descends into the canyon

  but I'm distracted by my lack of a question—any question —

and then the line has drooped and dissolved

into the chasm's ambush of air.

No incision anymore between dark and light.

The canyon goes fuzzy bright, dark and light at once

which is mostly what they're like, questions.

But I promise : the dark is as transparent as the light.

And from the windy knit of day, my mother texts, *are you leaving soon?*

The truth is, I am. I'll ask no more questions.

Gone mooring, throne, coil—where *eye-language* crumbles

and goes calmly cryptic unto itself.

No tremor, no invention. And I promise, no honesty.

The sky skulls. Droves of people die. Those less vulnerable ask what
    about Thanksgiving.

Each stone has unique specific gravity, crystal form, tenacity,
    luster, cleavage.

Each stone differently holds density, shape, survival, shine, breakage.

How it breaks : *perfect in two directions at right angles to each other /*
    perfect in one direction / a rhomboidal parting / very perfect, tastes
    like salt / prismatic, tabular, sub-translucent / adamantine,
    metallic, non-combustible—

I place a small, unremarkable stone upon a grave.

All my history and prediction, all my churn-bred sheen.

Doggedness borne of bewilderment, trying to outwit my script.

I can't.

I'm back graveside with that stone, back with the *Kaddish*, the same prayer
    Rosalie couldn't remember while in the death camp. Though it's a
    prayer for the dead, death is never mentioned. It's a praise song
    for the gift of life, for having lived.

You don't so much say it for

the dead—the dead

speak through you. You, the pray-er, are proxy, portal, for the dead
    you recall.

Maybe it will seem odd to you to think of filling a solid mass with nothing.

Blue arrives. I am arrived by blue.

Wrung out and tired by my internal spin, I put my head squarely inside
    the noose

spun by all that spinning.

Nothing is going to happen, says the noose.

Ein sof: "nothing." Also a term for god.

...

My eyes keep closing. So maybe I'll close my eyes. Outweighed by
    tiredness, I lie down on top of the covers wrapped in the wool
    shirt. I count my breaths, try to anticipate nothing.

I fail. Get up, go to the kitchen, heat up old coffee. It explodes inside the
    microwave. All the books' pages flap open to wrong parts. My
    eyes keep closing. The heater isn't heating right. Retaliatory
    matter. The day is a splendor of latches and barbs. I'm being
    spit out.

...

After decades of marriage, my friend wonders aloud
almost generously, with the remoteness of pure grief
bestowed by the totality of her former husband's plunder—
How can someone I thought I knew so well...

It's been asked so many times before but — What

                          do we ever know

        about another person? What

            have I ever known

        about another person?

       The not-self remains.

The intimate heat/alien heat

and scent of particular skin.

This may be all that's knowable so all that's ever known.

Ferocious immediacy, sinew of feeling, a thread made of memory

       and sensory flare.

Its mica-bright sparkle for a moment if we glance

while looking also away. I wake

a hundred times each night, eyes swiveling

daring back the dark to see

me : unity, moorage, sewn in perforation, perfectly strewn —

...

Life expectancy :

a tempting thread

to trace but really

the thread's

length

shape

survival

shine

breakage

how it breaks—

is visible only

in who or what

it punctures

how it becomes a seam.

a canyon

is a type of tear

made into a seam by

sun's bright thread

moon's lucent thread

stars' glinting, many threads

wind's transparent, endless threads

sensate animal threads

accurate animal threads

insects' threads whirring

threads of the junipers' writhe

threads

unspooling

through the canyon

sewing a shared seam

looping

remaking

both

story

&

sight

Sky doesn't skull today, it waxes pale blue.

Blue begins to show again what's black mesa, what's black hill.

Yesterday I cried on both the river's bridges, forehead braced

against iron bridge beams. The river pulled

the cry from me. A knowing being known.

Erotic : absolute contact between self / not-self

The erotic is the nurturer or nursemaid of all our deepest knowledge.

Blue sunrise, erotic. River-cry, erotic.

Today I knew exactly where and when the gold light

would gild the mesa's lip.

This place has taught me its moves

taught me how to feel them become me.

Emplacement is erotic.

Not-self, self : we become

what we can't recover from.

To recover is, at least partly, to conceal.

To pray is to mix wonder and danger, to wager, to stray.

Do I move toward form, do I use all my fears?

On my last lap around the track

the sun fully crests the eastern mesa

and heat begins to pool with landed light.

I don't move into the mesa's cool shadow.

I'm warmed and fully lit

when I turn a hard left, west, heading home.

3 / RETURN TO THE WESTERN EDGE

Where am I? My fingers are freezing.

I can't feel the ocean. The ocean is right there.   *But what is this mixture*

of mutiny and stringent peace

By which I feel, inside myself, the volatile discordance of the world?

But what is this fierce chemistry

that keeps my life in its groove, gives the groove sway.

I try to stay suspended, as between

the chair and the couch,

the window and the bed,

the school track in Winnemucca and the cold Oregon coast,

between hunger and absence,

stridency and tremor,

tenderness and breaking clear into a sprint —

as if all is outstretched,

as if I could just keep walking,

making wrong articulations in a slippery socket,

broken and healed in ways that trace the breakage,

make a gait that swerves

like a river or a river-bound road.

The dividings. The divinations. The differences between.

It isn't until later that I'll know what any of this means.

Why the grass's green stings to see.

I stare at the overflowing trash, coffee grounds on yesterday's plastic.

Matter sags wetly into itself.

The wholly sodden forest, dripping thick with dew,

moss-swelled, lichen-laced, a cold, wet fingertip

held to the candle of the desert's total spark, its death dance, snuffed.

              I know, I knew... a different mysticism

          in the green mold. I try to feel it, fail.

     Forced air, cold dew, gray light to dampen

the mind's ceaseless spin, bog it, seal its cinders.

The exit is through ash.

The exit is a throughline I've walked before, and blindly.

Careful hands at helpless hips, close-hewn with shadows.

Visitation, overthrow, a tearing of fluid apart.

What holds the shadow still holds.

The chaos I bring / the chaos I displace —

I try to triangulate, constellate imprisonment, look for a looking back.

At home, in bed, confused. Estranged by familiarity.
The medium-black spider that was living in my kitchen
is still living in my kitchen.
Sun has risen in Ojito Canyon. Streetlight time here.
Who knows what type of dark it is
       when lights are always on.

       My mind races laps around the shortfalls of matter—

       Power lines decussate thick gray.

       I guess this is dawn. Gray gone somewhat paler.

       Six crows cawing south.

       The vicissitudes of stasis.   Restive bodies inside routine.

The waves, plainly patterned but—

       their undertow.

Tiny birds chirp in the neighbor's mossy quince.
I consider near-endless permutations, settle again on simple
       devastation,

deployed into a war to find out how

to do anything other than fight.

Keep the discord. Keep the edge, it will be center

soon. Shapeshifter, poised relation, everything hewn here.

When I left, there were red maple leaves, dogwood leaves gone gold.

All leafless now. Branches.   A branch is a structure of

dormancy/sustenance

seeking/stasis

rigidity/bending

interiority/appendage —

branches hold me : aorta, spine.   Breath is a type

of branching.

Invoke, forge, locate.   The day is a dated map.

The day is a bright contraction.

A clench of cold light.

What's not to love about a good hiding spot

in this boundless game of seek.

What's not to love about customary suffering

that can't quite be seen.

make my heart more corpuscular than muscular — as in the corpuscular

theory of light, Descartes, 1637 :   light is made of corpuscles :

diminutive particles   that travel in straight lines

have finite velocity   and possess impetus.

Give my heart impetus, let it possess velocity, predilection.

A muscle mostly remembers.

I watch Circle Creek speed to the sea.

My shoulder muscles fill with rivers of volition.

Whose impetus? Whose line?

...

Dense fog. An SUV passes just outside my window in a clot of noise.

Indigo clouds shed fat drops. Chalky light slants between cloud slabs,
        swift in the cold above the city's grid.

A hawk's persistent, high cry from the tip of a tall fir : *the remembered
        home is not one home but clusters*

of otherwise and absence, reeling, ever-changing. Nor is here one single here.

How the I constantly crumbles yet still stands.

Crevices of sight align with crevices of memory. Overlaid
transparencies adding up to fog.

The jaw justifies its jut.

The cat watches the gray. 8:04 on a Tuesday morning and my brain
wants out.

The brain's improper funerals. The brain's mistranslations.

If any law runs through matter, the brain neutralizes it, makes it bleed
refraction.

Measure this anxious banter with the lodestar of gray or with the
morning sun turning only halfway on like when the movie's
credits roll, show's over.

...

I drive my car straight into the wind, into the air's intent.

Crows flap east into pink intent. Into powerline-sliced sky.

Sunrise, an imperative. Wind shakes the door on its flimsy hinges.

If I were a gully or a plain.

Below happiness, hypnosis.

To the west and to the east, mountains loom imperious, sheer and
beyond a need for love.

Take, god said, your child up high and kill him there.

Loops of the garbage truck round and round the block, tightening
loops of logic's noose, squeezing nothing.

Nothing, the summative voice. The aggregate, untamed.

Nothing, the conjoined eccentricity of all eccentric orbits.

Here I am again, doing Nothing, pushing sutures to the surface of
what cannot close.

...

Morning moon, a pliant confusion in a crisp sky.

The shower fills the room with steam, breathing across the windows, a
long exhale that the city's wind breathes in.

The moon is a fingernail that tore softly off, leaving furred sinew,
bone's softer words.

Black electric lines frame Venus. I cross out "electric," write "power."
The words are far from synonymous. By the time I finish trying to
trace that trade and look again, Venus is subsumed
inside the sentence.

The sentence now holds time, Venus, electric, power, and their
incongruous sum.

The habit of small focus : a machine gone helpless with function.

Pebbled clouds peach now, lavender-backed and strewn.

Friends call me, concerned by my absence. I don't call back, though I
  love them back.

Two obsidian stones atop a broken speaker. Fires in the river valleys
  blanketed now in snow.

The war began far away but soon entered our ears. The war was just down
the street when it began to move my face into shapes I could not
read. The war found in me a puppet and a stage.

The war played.

The war stayed.

The war ate anything that resembled silence. Ate birds, too. The
tiny ones first, downy gray feathers still matted with fog. But
soon the goshawks and the egrets. Even the albatross, her
acreaged wings.

Disappearance tumbled over itself to disappear.

What is the part of us that feels it isn't named, that doesn't know

How to respond to any name?

The jay pecking the black rocks expects to have hands, expects hands
every day,

is bewildered by her blue wings, surprised by how they
offer freedom

but disallow holding or being firmly held.

Surprised, too, by the efficacy of her wings

as tools for making distance, the way they slice precisely

into air in order to be of it.

I try to close. This must be done to avoid being named.

...

A scant mile from my house, the pre-dawn highway blares its sound into
the dark, a raucous void of noise. The sound swallows, tamps and
hollows. Birds shift the timbre of their songs, copy their
captor's sound.

The sound sounds a clear instruction : leave. *There exist ways of listening
the listener hardly understands.* You don't need to know what is
right in order to move steadily toward it.

All the ways I've tried to love this place.

The plants rooted here, returning each year.

Metronome perception, swung far out.

I keep reappearing here
      hoping to appear.   The world
          means exactly
what it means and
       is also always
         storied   doubled
   refracted back.

               How to navigate
      this luminous how
to start each day in the dark.
    Birds remain wild
      you said.   right in front of us
               The world means
  exactly
what it means
     I said. Then you said   witness, hive.

Our disappearance, though
   certain, is only relatively
        imminent.   Can a hunger
   be so lucid
     that it is its own   reward.
Can a hunger be clasp or loam.

             Can a hunger be
    so cogent
  that its home is migration.
  What if this is it.   The end.
              What if the
              hunger's hunger is

only to remain, to fly across the same knot
    trace it over again   to re-form

             the question.

— middle of a room, middle of a grid, eyes whirling

where are the edges of the self —

caged alone and the compass

stutters into spin. I pile books
around me, open portals. The map grew again through a lock. *One is
several, incomplete, and subject to dispersal.*

In the portals, I find voices I love. Voices of love.
My own voice cast back off anyone else's skin : their languages love
me back. I allow them to become me, let languages overlap.

Whose afterimage am I? Our ghosts cannot be ousted.

When I fell off my bike and my hip hit ice, my instinct was to
jump up quick, pretend I wasn't hurt. I was hurt. I leave my husband
for another love and then that love leaves me. To stretch my hurt hip, I
was taught to stretch my shoulders : *Do you even know / what part of you
you are?*

'Something before that, with no name.'

clasp or loam

Can a hunger be

the entire west burning. Flames singe my memory, my home,
turn it all to ash.
I'm poised ready to flee, almost eager : certainty is ridiculous

— while flash bangs and copters

blight acrimonious air. Traps, traps, traps. Federal agents, unmarked
cars. Virulent orange nights. Battalions of Trump trucks slither
through town, hiss menace and venom in ash.

I leave, canyon-bound. A bright,
dry red I've never seen before.

My life, my place, my mind — clawed, winnowed from belief
back to path :

tras la rosa / sombra

beyond the rose / shadow

Can a hunger be

mooring, throne, coil — the dividings. The divinations.
The differences between.

The bright pliancy of human sentience — attention itself —

                                        porous boundaries, our bodies cannot be

considered apart from the stories we tell of them.

                    I tell this path as it was walked, as it was incanted.

         Wholesale burnishing, wholesale cracking up, wholesale

                                   vanishing of mind

'Something before that, with no name.' No naming.

                     Dissolution, gift — driven by a soft motor other

than a mind

              re-arrayed by time.

                         Whenever I say "I" I mean also "you". And
                              so, together, as one, we shall begin

      to keep the body, the hunger, the hunger looking back.

NOTES

Thank you to the following poets, writers, artists, philosophers, scientists, and journalists whose words comprise the chorus without which this book would not exist. Your words kept me alive.

EPIGRAPH

Lyn Hejinian: *One is several, incomplete, and subject to dispersal.*

Alice Notley: *Do you even know / what part of you you are?*

Ayad Akhtar: *...The bright pliancy of human sentience — attention itself — had become the world's most prized commodity, the very movements of our minds transformed into streams of unceasing revenue for someone, somewhere.*

Bayo Akomolafe: *In this epoch of porous boundaries, our bodies cannot be considered apart from the stories we tell of them.*

Nietzsche: *Let us beware of saying that death is opposed to life. The living is only a form of what is dead, and a very rare form.*

Blanca Varela: *Después // tras la rosa / sombra*

W. S. Merwin: *The story of the one-legged messenger is that his other leg is walking on the far side of death. 'What seems to be over there?' they ask him. 'Just emptiness?' 'No,' he says. 'Something before that, with no name.'*

William Carlos Williams: *Whenever I say "I" I mean also "you". And so, together, as one, we shall begin.*

CHORUS 1

Jorie Graham: *other scenes are not taking place*

CHORUS 2

Laurie Sheck: *So much elsewhere unsettling each surface, so much annulled.*

CHORUS 3

Carl Phillips: *complete because of its tensions*

CHORUS 4

Carl Phillips: *elsewise*

CHORUS 5

Camilo Mora: *"'Somebody asked me if there is a good ending to the horror movie,' Dr. Mora said. 'The good ending was 20 years ago. Now, the choices for the ending are 'bad' and 'terrible'. The planet, it's screaming to us,' he said. 'When are we going to start listening?'"*

Laurie Sheck: *of mutiny and stringent peace*

CHORUS 6

Gillian Conoley: *there is no time but the light remains*

Charles Olson: *what does not change is the will to change*

CHORUS 7

William Carlos Williams: *surely in isolation one becomes a god*

CHORUS 8

Laurie Sheck: *most curious to me the visible world in that it has no motive*

CHORUS 9

Joseph Conrad: *All this is life, must be life, since it is so much like a dream. ... truth stripped of its cloak of time*
Imbecile rapacity

Laurie Sheck: *Thinking is a truceless act.*

CHORUS 10

Aria Aber: *I thought, If only the eye wasn't the harbinger of forgiveness.*

CHORUS 11

Laurie Sheck: *elsewhere of water*

Michel Serres: *What is closed? What is open? What is a connective path? [...] What is a threshold, a limit?*

José Lezama Lima: *from pore to star*

CHORUS 12

Laurie Sheck: *vast inexplicable*

CHORUS 13

Laurie Sheck: *as when an otherwise / Opens in the body*

Lia Purpura: *No plan, just belief.*

CHORUS 14

Laurie Sheck: *habitable scars*

Mark Strand: *in a field / I am the absence / of field*

CHORUS 15

Gillian Conoley: *There is no time but the light remains.*

Laurie Sheck: *shockwaves of the mind slides as fever in the veins*

CHORUS 16

Laurie Sheck: *hurt pathways of thought*

Robert MacFarlane: *Footfall as knowledge*

CHORUS 17

Etel Adnan: *Water brings energy the way memory creates identity. One's life is one's home.*

CHORUS 18
Carl Phillips: *To see a thing only for what it physically is, is its own distortion.*

CHORUS 19
Laurie Sheck: *A rough and intricate hazard*
So many plurals and veerings, so much away

Gertrude Stein: *If anything is alive there is no such thing as repetition.*

CHORUS 20
Karen Barad: *exuberant transience*

Gillian Conoley: *made as we are of molecules and lament / where an intelligence lives.*

CHORUS 21
Mei-Mei Berssenbrugge: *fragile imaginal cloth holding*
Everything arrives energetically, at first.

Diane di Prima: *every man/every woman carries a firmament inside / & the stars in it are not the stars in the sky.*

CHORUS 22
Mei-Mei Berssenbrugge: *fragile imaginal*
Stars are holes in the dark; when I look at one, I go there; entity contact eases emotion.

CHORUS 23
Robert Macfarlane: *In the dusk of the holloways, these pasts felt excitingly alive and coexistent - as if time had somehow pleated back on itself, bringing discontinuous moments into contact, and creating historical correspondences that survived as a territorial imperative to concealment and escape.*

Michael Taussig: *between meaning and force, between the idea and a body*

CHORUS 24

Glossary of Cartographic Terms: *By following the sinuousities of the bank or shoreline, the meander line provides data for computing the area of land remaining after the water area has been segregated. [... A meander line] does not ordinarily determine or fix boundaries.*

Lia Purpura: *I'm getting rearranged by all the seeing and being seen.*

Clayton Eshleman: *no way / to predetermine reception*

Kenneth Rexroth: *silent, vertiginous sliding*

CHORUS 25

Etel Adnan: *Knowledge of the void is knowledge of fullness.*

CHORUS 26

Mei-Mei Bersenbrugge: *gravity, allure, origin*

Jed Rasula: *a realm superseding individual volition*

Heidegger: *Thrownness*

Harold Bloom: *What is known knows the knower.*

Gomes de Zurara: *lived like beasts, without any custom of reasonable beings . . . [and] only knew how to live in bestial sloth.*

Ruby Nell Sales: *Soul murder*
Is it a privilege to inherit a death-driven system

Derek Jarman: *Gray surrounds us and we ignore it.*

CHORUS 27

Laurie Sheck: *what consoles does wondering console*

CHORUS 28

Jerome Rothenberg: *Let the earth drop away inside your belly falling falling until you're left in space*

Michael Palmer: *Write this. A word may be shaped like a bed, a basket or tears or an X*

CHORUS 29
Laurie Sheck: *eye-language*

CHORUS 30
George Letchworth English and David E. Jensen:
perfect in two directions at right angles to each other...
Maybe it will seem odd to you to think of filling a solid mass with nothing.

CHORUS 31
Georgia O'Keefe: *I realized I had things in my head not like what I had been taught — not like what I had seen — shapes and ideas so familiar to me that it hadn't occurred to me to put them down. I decided to stop painting, to put away everything I had done, and to start to say the things that were my own.*

CHORUS 32
Audre Lorde: *[The erotic is]...the first and most powerful guiding light toward any understanding. And understanding is a handmaiden which can only wait upon or clarify, that knowledge, deeply born. The erotic is the nurturer or nursemaid of all our deepest knowledge.*

Muriel Rukeyser: *Do I move toward form, do I use all my fears?*

CHORUS 33
Laurie Sheck: *But what is this mixture of mutiny and stringent peace...*

CHORUS 34
Guy Debord: *The spectacle in general, as the concrete inversion of life, is the autonomous movement of the non-living.*

CHORUS 35

b: william bearhart: *make my heart more corpuscular than muscular.*

Laurie Sheck: *the remembered home is not one home but clusters / of otherwise and absence, reeling, ever-changing. Nor is here one single here. / How the I constantly crumbles yet still stands.*

CHORUS 36

Lia Purpura: *There exist ways of listening the listener hardly understands.*

Laurie Sheck: *What is the part of us that feels it isn't named, that doesn't know / How to respond to any name?*

CHORUS 37

Paul Preciado: *Our disappearance, though certain, is only relatively imminent.*

CHORUS 38

See epigraph

Aber, Aria. "An Essay on Loss" in Poetry, Don Share, editor, vol. 217, no. 4, January 2021.

Adnan, Etel. *Night*. Nightboat Books, 2016.

Akhtar, Ayad. *Homeland Elegies: A Novel*. Little, Brown and Company, 2020.

Akomolafe, Bayo. "When You Meet the Monster, Anoint Its Feet." *Emergence Magazine*. Accessed May 18 2020. https://emergencemagazine.org/story/when-you-meet-the-monster/

Barad, Karen. "On Touching the Stranger Within – The Alterity that therefore I Am." *The Poetry Project*. https://www.poetryproject.org/publications/poems-texts/on-touching

bearheart, b: william. "No More Fire Here: A Sestina" Academy of American Poets. https://poets.org/poem/no-more-fire-here-sestina

Bersenbrugge, Mei Mei. *A Treatise on Stars*. New Directions, 2020.

Bloom, Harold. *Agon: Towards a Theory of Revisionism*. Oxford University Press, 1982.

Conoley, Gillian. *A Little More Red Sun on the Human*. Nightboat Books, 2019.

Conrad, Joseph. *Heart of Darkness*. Tuttle Publishing, 1995.

Debord, Guy. *Society of the Spectacle*. Black and Red, 2002.

de Zurara, Gomes. *The Chronicle of the Discovery and Conquest of Guinea*. Cambridge University Press, 2010.

di Prima, Diane. "Rant" http://modampo.blogspot.com/2006/04/diane-di-primas-rant.html

English, George Letchworth and David E. Jensen. *Getting Acquainted with Minerals*. Gwendolyn English Burleson and David E. Jensen, 1958.

Eshelman, Clayton. *Antiphonal Swing: Selected Prose, 1962-1987*. Mc Pherson, 1989.

"Glossary of Cartographic Terms" University of Texas Libraries. https://legacy.lib.utexas.edu/maps/glossary.html

Graham, Jorie. "Poem" in *Poetry*, Don Share, editor, vol. 215, no. 4, January 2020.

Hejinian, Lyn. *The Language of Inquiry*. University of California Press, 2000.

Jarman, Derek. *Chroma*. University Of Minnesota Press, 2010.

Lezama Lima, José. "*Orbita* Interview." James Irby, translator. *Sulfur* 24, 1989, p. 172-83.

Lorde, Audre. *The Selected Works of Audre Lorde*. W. W. Norton, 2020.

MacFarlane, Robert. *Underland*. W. W. Norton & Company, 2019.

Merwin, W.S. *The Book of Fables*. Copper Canyon Press, 2007.

Mora, Camilo. in "A season of climate-fueled disasters" by John Schwartz, September 16, 2020, *The New York Times*. https://www.nytimes.com/2020/09/16/climate/wildfires-hurricanes-climate-change.html

Nietzsche, Friedrich. *The Gay Science: With a Prelude in Rhymes and an Appendix of Songs*. Vintage, 1974.

Notley, Alice. *Descent of Alette*. Penguin, 1996.

O'Keefe, Georgia. *Some Memories of Drawings*. University of New Mexico Press, 1974.

Olson, Charles. "The Kingfishers" from *The Collected Poems of Charles Olson*. Regents of the University of California, 1987.

Palmer, Michael. *Sun*. North Point Press, 1988.

Phillips, Carl. *The Art of Daring: Risk, Restlessness, Imagination*. Graywolf Press, 2014.

—. *Wild is the Wind*. Farrar Straus & Giroux, 2018.

Preciado, Paul. *Countersexual Manifesto.* Columbia University Press, 2018.

Purpura, Lia. *All the Fierce Tethers.* Sarabande Books, 2019.

—. "The Creatures of the World Have Not Been Chastened." *Emergence Magazine.* https://emergencemagazine.org/story/the-creatures-of-the-world-have-not-been-chastened/

Rasula, Jed. *This Compost.* University of Georgia Press, 2002.

Rexroth, Kenneth. *The Complete Poems of Kenneth Rexroth.* Copper Canyon Press, 2004.

Rothenberg, Jerome. *Khurbn and Other Poems.* New Directions, 1989.

Rukeyser, Muriel. *The Life of Poetry.* Wesleyan University Press, 1996.

Sales, Ruby Nell. "Can We Just Get Down to the Conversation About Whiteness?" *The Shed.* https://theshed.org/program/147-help/additional-resources/ruby-nell-sales

Serres, Michel. *Genesis.* G. James and J. Nielson, translators. University of Michigan Press, 1982.

Sheck, Laurie. *Captivity.* Alfred A. Knopf, 2007.

Stein, Gertrude. "Portraits and Repetition." *Stein: Writings 1932-1946.* Penguin, 2001.

Strand, Mark. "Keeping Things Whole" from *Selected Poems.* Alfred A. Knopf, 1979.

Taussig, Michael. *What Color is the Sacred?* University of Chicago Press, 2009.

Varela, Blanca. *Rough Song.* The Song Cave, 2020.

Williams, William Carlos. *Spring and All.* New Directions, 1970.

ACKNOWLEDGMENTS

Thank you to Chris Kerr for featuring "chorus 21 / Ojito Canyon / storm" and "chorus 2" in "The Inner Forest Service" Issue 1, October 2021.

Thank you to Amy Harwood for featuring "chorus 18 / ojito canyon / election" in *The First 100 Days: Election Day 2020.*

THANK YOU

Kazim Ali and Omnidawn, thank you for believing in this work and for changing my life by doing so.

Mom, thank you for being and raising a writer.

Rosalie, for the haunting.

Thank you Dad, Gabe, David, Rachel, Ozzi, Miles, Eric, and my entire family, living and dead, present, past, and future.

Coy, for being most bammer.

Thank you to my cat Stir Fry aka Lord Kitty Potato aka Buddybuddy, etcetera, for his unconditional love and dignity (despite his names) and for always listening attentively to me when I read drafts aloud.

Eva, Billy, Devin, and Oliver at Mission Street Arts residency (Jemez Springs, New Mexico) thank you for making this book possible. It could not have been written without the welcoming, inspiring space you create in that canyon.

Thank you to my brilliant, generous poet friends who read drafts of this work and offered vital feedback: Tobi Kassim, Emmi Greer, and Liz Lampman.

Solmaz Sharif, Airea D. Matthews, Connie Voisine, and Sally Keith: Thank you, teachers, for all you've given and continue to give. I admire you.

Poetry Church congregants, thank you for your ongoing mentorship, laughter, and love: Sara Guest, Zachary Schomburg, and John Morrison.

Thanks to Sebastian Merrill, Dane Slutzky, Aaron Hauptman, Eric Cruz, and the entire community of dedicated writers and teachers at Warren Wilson College. And thank you, Brad, for helping make my time at Warren Wilson possible.

Thank you, friends — you have put up with my frequent disappearances and have made me a better human. Your stories appear in these pages: Julia, Roy, Amy, Tarp, Nina, Kaitlyn, Emily, Jay, Jeffrey...

Thank you to my students, for teaching me.

Thank you to the poets, scientists, philosophers, artists, journalists, and novelists whose words appear in these pages. "I want the spectator to be reassured that something he values within himself has been touched and found a kind of correspondence. That being alive [...] is worth the labor." — Clyfford Still

Thanks to an art school in Portland, Oregon, for being spectacularly fucked — jumping your sinking ship allowed this book to be written.

Thank you, dear reader, for joining the chorus.

I am grateful to the earth for sustaining life.

Daniela Naomi Molnar is an artist, poet, and writer working with the mediums of language, image, paint, pigment, and place. She is also a wilderness guide, educator, and eternal student. She can be found in Portland, Oregon, exploring public wildlands, or at www.danielamolnar.com
Instagram: @daniela_naomi_molnar

Chorus
by Daniela Naomi Molnar

Cover art by Daniela Naomi Molnar

Interior typeface: Garamond Premier Pro
Cover design by Daniela Naomi Molnar
Interior design by Ken Keegan and Daniela Naomi Molnar

Printed in the United States
by Books International, Dulles, Virginia
on Acid Free Archival Quality Recycled Paper

Publication of this book was made possible in part by gifts from Katherine
& John Gravendyk in honor of Hillary Gravendyk, Francesca Bell, Mary
Mackey, and The New Place Fund

Omnidawn Publishing
Oakland, California
Staff and Volunteers, Spring 2022

Rusty Morrison & Ken Keegan, senior editors & co-publishers
Laura Joakimson, production editor and poetry & fiction editor
Rob Hendricks, editor for Omniverse, poetry & fiction,
& post-pub marketing
Sharon Zetter, poetry editor & book designer
Jeff Kingman, copy editor
Liza Flum, poetry editor
Anthony Cody, poetry editor
Jason Bayani, poetry editor
Gail Aronson, fiction editor
Jennifer Metsker, marketing assistant
Jordyn MacKenzie, marketing assistant
Sophia Carr, marketing assistant